The Incredible Power of a Praying Woman

*A part of the
"Classics by the Archbishop"
Series*

Archbishop Nicholas Duncan-Williams

Copyright © 2009 by Archbishop Nicholas Duncan-Williams

The Incredible Power of a Praying Woman
by Archbishop Nicholas Duncan-Williams

Printed in the United States of America

ISBN 978-1-60034-405-3

All rights reserved solely by the author. The author guarantees all contents are original and do not infringe upon the legal rights of any other person or work. No part of this book may be reproduced in any form without the permission of the author. The views expressed in this book are not necessarily those of the publisher.

Unless otherwise indicated, Bible quotations are taken from the King James version of the Bible.

www.xulonpress.com

Table of Contents

Chapter 1	The Epidemic	11
Chapter 2	The Diagnosis	17
Chapter 3	Deceptive Symptoms in Our Camp	23
Chapter 4	Has the Devil Located You?	33
Chapter 5	The Pride of Life	43
Chapter 6	Many Christians Are Disillusioned	51
Chapter 7	The Cure for PWC	57
Chapter 8	The Ultimate Prayer Man	63

Introduction

As a woman you deal with a lot of emotions that sometimes cause stress. Many of these take place each month before and after the menstrual cycle. During these times, you may be prone to do things you would not normally do.

It is important that you are careful not to make decisions based on what you are feeling in your body or what your emotions dictate. If you respond to what you are feeling emotionally during these times, there is sometimes a tendency to be unstable and unpredictable. That kind of personality change can alter the character or even destabilize a person.

Women, you must realize that you are not a soul or a body, but a spirit. You must cultivate the attitude of training your soul to come into compliance with the dictates of your spirit. A lot of good men have left good women like you for other women who have learned this important principle.

Some of the problems you go through are in the soul. And until you learn how to master your soul, the enemy always will have an advantage over you. If you don't learn how to master your soul, you are destined to live a soulish life. A soulish life cannot prosper physically or spiritually because the soul is selfish and greedy. The soul is a bridge between the body and spirit. What comes through the spirit cannot get to the body unless it comes through the soul.

The soul is Satan's target. The battle is with the soul. That is why David said in Psalm 23, "He restoreth my soul." This scripture seems to imply that the soul can be damaged. I know many of you can identify with David because of traumas in your life. You may have been the victim of child abuse, rape, or incest, or perhaps in later years, you had an abortion. All these things, if not dealt with, can cause you to become angry, controlling, and manipulating.

The only way to avoid selfishness is to avoid living in the soul. To do that, you must walk in the spirit and live in the spirit. This is because the love of God is shed abroad in our spirit, not in our soul. The love of God is not soulish, it is spiritual. It is not a feeling or an emotion.

The key is found in James 5:13: "Is any among you afflicted? Let him pray." The definition of *afflict* is to trouble, sorrow, anguish, grieve, harm, hurt, injure, sadden, torment, upset, worry: to bring great harm or suffering to. Sometimes the result of what you are going through can subconsciously cause you to nag, complain, curse, whine, manipulate, overeat, cry, or become angry, frustrated, or even vindictive with your husband and children. Remember, "Neither give place to the devil" (Ephesians 4:27). You can, however, give him place subconsciously by holding on to these things. It is important to remember that you are a spirit, that you have a soul and live in a body.

The soul is comprised of the mind, will, and emotions. It is important for you to release yourself from the negative emotions, the stress, and the pressure you hold inside because you carry a lot of responsibility.

When the Bible says, "I will make him a help mate," it means women would complement the man. Women have different capabilities. They are able to endure more physical pain. Childbirth is probably the best example. Also, it has been biologically proven that women think with both hemispheres of their brain at any given time. Women are able to cook, talk on the phone, feed the children, and watch television at the same time. Men, on the other hand, think and concentrate on one thing at a time.

As a woman, God has given you incredible natural abilities to see what men often find difficult to detect. Your innate intuition is remarkable, and when channeled into prayer, you are bound to enjoy incredible results.

When the Bible says, "I will make him a help mate," it simply means that the woman makes the man complete. Women are only weaker in their physical makeup, but not in their spiritual makeup.

As a woman living in the twenty-first century, you are dealing with things that your mother and grandmothers did not necessarily have to deal with—everything from a career outside the home to managing the home and caring for the family. The pressure and stress, when unchecked, have become a leading cause of many of the ailments and diseases that women encounter today, including fibromyalgia, chronic fatigue syndrome, delusional guilt, postpartum psychosis, psychotic depression, major depressive disorder, psychosis, anxiety, and even filicide.

Isaiah 28:12 talks about "the rest wherewith ye may cause the weary to rest; and this is the refreshing." Don't be like the children of Israel, who, Scripture says, "would not hear." God has given you a way of escape, found in Romans 8:26 and Jude 1:20.

Your answer is found in prayer. By praying in tongues, you are able to solve your problems. The Bible says to build up your faith by praying in the Holy Ghost. I pray in tongues to edify myself. Self-edification—that is the key.

Women, you must pray when you are taking the children to school, when they come home, and at all other times. It is good to play Christian music, but that will not do for you what prayer will do. Christian music ministers primarily to your soul. There are times when you need something deeper. You need to touch God. Praying in the Spirit is one of the most powerful weapons. Paul said, "I pray with understanding, I pray with the spirit" but when he prays with unknown tongues he speaks not to man but to God. So keep talking to God. Whenever you pray in the Spirit, you build yourself up. You will feel peace inside, and you will not be irritated, angry, revengeful, or vindictive.

The key is adhering to the Scripture solution. You will never succeed otherwise. Because of the times in which you live, with all the pressure, you cannot continue to solve your problems emotionally; you may not survive. You must get into the Spirit. You have to move in the Spirit.

Look at Queen Esther. The fate of her entire nation rested upon her shoulders. Esther's actions would determine the future of all of Israel (you cannot have much more pressure or stress than that); yet look at how she responded. When her uncle Mordecai told her about the plot and the impending destruction of the Jews by Hamaan, Esther did not react emotionally, go to the king by her beauty, or use sex or her charm. Esther was sensitive to the Spirit. She was not foolish; she did not act based on her emotions. Instead she was depending on the Spirit through prayer and fasting; ultimately, God gave her the victory.

If you are familiar with the story of Hannah in 1 Samuel 1, you will remember the adversity that Hannah endured. Her husband, Elkanah, was also married to Peninnah, a woman who had borne him several children, while Hannah remained barren.

Hannah endured everything—from social embarrassment and the stigma associated with it—to constant provoking from her rival. Hannah had good reason to feel discouraged and bitter. After all, in her society, she was a social outcast. She could have retaliated against Peninnah or blamed her husband and made life miserable for him, but instead Hannah took her problem to God in prayer.

Each of another, or us, at one time has faced times of barrenness when nothing seems to come to birth, whether it is in a relationship, in our work, or in our service. But one thing that we must learn is that prayer opens the way for God to work.

So what are you going to do? Will you continue to endure all that you have been going through, or will you pray? It is my prayer that by the time you finish reading this book, you will receive an impartation to pray.

-Archbishop N. Duncan-Williams

Chapter One:

The Epidemic

In my book, *The Supernatural Powers of a Praying Man*, I talk about the Ebola virus. You may never have heard of this deadly virus because it was contained before it could reach the Western world. The Ebola virus is a type of viral hemorrhagic fever. Symptoms begin four to sixteen days after infection. Once the symptoms—fever, chills, headache, muscle ache and loss of appetite—begin, the disease can take out its victim in less than seventy-two hours.

As this disease progresses, its symptoms also progress to include vomiting, diarrhea, abdominal pain, sore throat, and chest pain. With the rapid spread of the virus, a victim's blood eventually fails to clot, causing him or her to bleed from injection sites, the gastrointestinal tract, skin, and other organs.

Another sort of outbreak in our camp is equally awful. It affects a part of you and quickly spreads like the Ebola virus, attacking and destroying the vital organs that keep our bodies functioning. I call this virus Prayerlessness Without Ceasing, or PWC.

It contrasts Jesus' command to pray without ceasing. Unlike the Ebola virus, whose host is unknown, PWC has several hosts, some of which are manipulation, anger, rebellion, busy schedules, indifference, stubbornness, and pride. It is subtle and attacks from within and without. It weaves a gradual web of deceit around its victim and spreads to other parts of the body—in this case, the body of Christ.

This disease ends up trapping its victims into a prison of prayerlessness. The intricate weave of this web makes it almost impossible for one to free herself once caught in its trap. The symptoms of PWC can easily go undetected.

PWC weaves itself into the fabric of overly busy lives. This virus of prayerlessness is not partial; it is an equal opportunity virus. It does not care whether you stand in the office of president or bishop, janitor or general. Its main purpose is to throw other activities seemingly more pressing than prayer your way. PWC will weaken your mind first and trick you into believing that God is indifferent and understands your busy schedule. He may, but the devil will use it as an opportunity to lure you to his ways.

That is why as wives, mothers, and career women who find there is little time for anything beyond your duties in these roles, you can't let the devil into your lives. With the changing times, women are now faced with responsibilities and load that society once considered taboo. Women may be doing as much as men these days in terms of supporting the family and have a responsibility to maintain their homes and families. With the weight of the schedule of a present-day woman, how much time does she have to seek God?

As a woman, it is imperative that you find a secret place you can retreat to and fall on your face before God, a place where the enemy cannot touch you, a place where you wage war against the enemy and his plot against you. You need to maintain balance and remember that an unjust weight is an abomination to God. Beware of imbalances caused by an overemphasis on one form of worship at the expense of another.

There are several forms of worship. We worship God through songs, through giving ourselves to the work of the ministry, through studying the Bible and so on. In our efforts to please God in all these areas, we unfortunately forget the object that bridges the gap between God and us—the vehicle of prayer. The only way to combat the disease of prayerlessness is to pray, just as the only way to quench your thirst is to drink water.

I detect imbalance in churches today because an overemphasis on other forms of worship has left the scale tipping where prayer is concerned. Prayer has been pushed to the bottom of the priority list and is left to a few people on the prayer team pursue.

The same attitude has crept into our personal lives. We are gradually losing our sense of the importance of prayer. Prayer is for everyone, and to think it can be done once in a while when disaster strikes is a pity.

Sometimes we hide under the cloak of worship and replace prayer with worship. However, we need balance. When the enemy attacks, you cannot sing him away. You cannot quote him scriptures on finances and expect him to flee if he is attacking your children or your emotions. We are steadily losing our crucial and only connection to God, which is prayer.

As leaders of the millennium church, we have placed undue emphasis on music, praise, worship, finances, and marketing strategies, and have ignored prayer. We have taught the church to worship, to quote Scripture, to name it and claim it, but we have failed to teach the core part of our Christian walk, which is praying. Prayer is the cord that keeps us connected to the Father, but this imbalance has produced a generation of lawless and prayerless men and women who are not connected to their source.

A Fast-Paced Society Worsens the Epidemic

The hustle and bustle of our world today doesn't make it easy to spend time with God. Everything is fast-paced, and there is a quick fix for everything. The information/computer age has increased the pace of life more than a notch. There is a broken gadget that some super glue cannot fix. Manual labor has been replaced with the touch of a button, and everything can happen as and when you want it—now. Anything that requires waiting is a pressure task, and it irritates us. Even our kids have no time to stop and breathe. Society has robbed our future leaders of the virtue of patience.

Spending time with God can sometimes be a daunting task, if not altogether impossible, in light of our daily schedules. The phone rings, the pager goes off, the kids need to be picked up from school, your nails need to be done, and your hair appointment is somewhere in between. Somehow God gets left in between the to-do list and the pressing errands that spring up so easily as our day progresses.

Take a deep breath and slow down. There's a stop light ahead. There's a waiting period until the light turns green. Impatience will not work well if you are going to take up your God-given responsibility of praying ceaselessly.

Here's a funny story about patience. My older daughter was recently going through a tough period in her life, as do many young adults. As a graduate student out on her own, she often is faced with tough decisions and choices that she knows will alter the course of her life. Recently, she was faced with a particularly tough situation and needed a quick fix from God. As the pressure mounted, God seemed ever so silent.

One evening during that time, my daughter went to a Chinese restaurant with her friends, and as they ate dinner, she had a thought. God could speak to her through a fortune cookie. She quickly grabbed one from the table to see what the Lord had to say to her. The fortne cookie said, "You need to be patient," the exact words I said to her when she shared her challenges with me. She's had enough training in the Word to know that one needs to wait on God when in doubt, but the pressure sent her searching for the Word of God in the wrong place.

What is the pressure of waiting doing to you? Are you calling the psychic hotline when no one is looking in hopes that the Lord will give you a word? Watch out! You are walking in the devil's territory. Is the pressure of waiting for a godly spouse too much that sex on the Internet has become your source of release? Maybe lately your husband is giving you more problems than you ever anticipated you would have in your marriage, and your children are equally problematic.

When the pressure of life strikes, what is your source of release? How do you face the issues to which you have no solution or answer? Do you seek out the prophets in the land and try to twist God's arm for a word, or do you simply thrust yourself into His everlasting arms? There is a word that comes to those who wait on God. He may not give you the solution to your problem\, but He may simply give you enough strength to pull through until He's ready to unveil the mystery of His will.

Sometimes we feel beat and vulnerable when we are faced with the strange hurricanes and tornadoes of life. We give everyone the impression that we know what we are doing when sometimes they can clearly see we are lost and in need of help.

You don't need to cover up. You need to come clean and tell it like it is. God is not impressed with your strength. He is touched by your vulnerability. So stop, take a minute, and regroup. What is so difficult about admitting your weakness to God? He is a loving Father. Like me, you may not have experienced the love and protection of your natural father as a child. Don't close the door to God, for He is unlike your natural father. He will never leave nor forsake you, and your weaknesses only give Him an opportunity to show His strength.

Chapter Two:

The Diagnosis

If PWC has taken over your body, diagnose the problem and fight back. The time has come for women to rise up, to go back to the basics, and learn how to prevail through prayer before God. We talk about how our grandmother and our mothers prayed, how they stayed on their knees until situations changed. We are famous for remembering our grandmothers' prayers, but we are lacking in mimicking them. If your grandma prayed so consistently, why not follow her example by becoming an example for your grandchildren to talk about and be encouraged by? Grandma always knew how to go before the altar and stay there until God gave her an answer.

Some of you are where you are in God because of her prayers. There is more power when you fall on your face in prayer than in the most powerful atomic missile. Think about Esther, Hannah, and other women in the Bible who survived in the midst of difficult circumstances through the vehicle of prayer.

Women have an advantage in prayer because they understand what it means to travail. That's because travailing is an integral part of childbirth. If a woman wants to have natural birth, she must push. The same applies to prayer. Surrounding the birth of any miracle is the ability to push with travailing and persistent prayers. You must stand in the gap without wavering and pray until something happens. God does answer prayers. But the devil also hinders the results of our prayers. That is why we must learn how to stay consistent in prayer. We must learn how to pray and touch the heart of God. This is the only way we can defy the odds and challenge our adverse circumstances.

The Bible provides proof. It is graced with the names of women who changed circumstances through prayer. We see how these women walked in wisdom, the wisdom of God. Take, for example, Abigail. She was married to Nabal, a wicked and rather foolish man. Was Abigail happy? It's doubtful. She was aware of who her husband was. However, Abigail was delivered from her wicked husband and given to King David.

The wisdom Abigail received to overcome her circumstances came from God. She had prophetic insight that she could not have had if she did not know how to pray.

Deborah, a great woman of God, is the first female judge recorded in the Bible. Her great works continue to speak of her. She encouraged mighty men of God and assisted them in battle. She could have had that kind of strength and tenacity only through a personal relationship with God and through prayer. Another woman in the Bible, Hannah, made time to consistently seek God until she changed her circumstances, which ultimately changed her history.

Prayer is a vehicle through which we can come to know God. We know God by studying His Word and by spending time with Him. We spend time with Him by staying on our knees in prayer. Through God, many women in the Bible had the ability to overcome the extraordinary circumstances they faced.

What then is the problem with many Christian women today? Were the women of old more favored in the sight of God than women today? No. The difference is that women of old made time for God. They knew how to achieve their goals through persistence and determination. You cannot walk in the consistency and determination they walked in except through prayer and by a personal relationship with God.

There is urgency in the realm of the spirit for balance. If you are to make it in these times, prayer must be the key. The greatest form of power is not found in "girl power"—miniskirts, seduction, manipulation, or sex—it is found in the woman who has made prayer her secret habitation. This woman abides continually under the shadow of the Most High. She is covered. Show me a woman who is calm in the midst of storms, and I will show you a woman of prayer, for she knows that the supernatural controls the natural. How can the two walk together unless they agree, and how can they agree unless they communicate?

A relationship with God can be compared to a relationship with a spouse. A married couple cannot survive without the fundamental requirement of communication in their relationship. Couples who do not have good communication are walking in frustration. They may have a two-million-dollar house, a fleet of expensive cars, and a billion-dollar business. However, if they lack communication, their monumental wealth cannot save them. If you go beyond the boundaries that protect the house, you will find a couple struggling to survive.

Similarly, the mark of a great coach or leader is his ability to interact and communicate effectively with his team. He knows just what the team members need to become motivated because he has taken time to know and understand them. The importance of communication stretches way beyond these examples. In fact, the more effective communication is between any two people, the greater the bond they share. This is why we need to go down on our knees in prayer to God.

The mark of a prayerful woman is that she is in control of that which God has entrusted to her. Her battles are not fought in the natural but in the spirit. She understands that the spiritual rules the natural and that the battle is not hers but God's. She is a comfort to her husband in trying times. Her insight and advice only builds and never tears down. A praying woman is priceless.

It takes a praying woman to overcome feelings of insecurity, anger, depression, and the desire to manipulate others to favor her course. She is in tune with her Creator, and her natural instincts are sharpened to detect the foulest of deals. The praying woman doesn't sleep her way to the top or destroy others for her own gain. She simply tackles her issues through the conduit of prayer. This does not mean that a prayerful woman doesn't confront issues. Instead, she handles and confronts issues with godly wisdom. The book of

James encourages us to ask for wisdom if we lack it. Wisdom does not come because we desire it. Wisdom comes because we ask for it in prayer.

Women have a head start when it comes to praying. They just need to follow through. There is a God-given desire in women to pray. Organize a prayer meeting, and women will fill the seats. Women have a unique ability to touch the heart of God through prayer. It is incredible to watch women pray. Giving one's self in prayer is such an easy task for a woman.

I encourage you to get yourself back on your knees. If you have never been on your knees consistently, there is no better time to start than now. We read books on prayer and get motivated to pray effectively for a day or two, and then slip back into prayerlessness. I sometimes wonder how we find time for everything else, but can hardly find the time to pray. There's nothing wrong with taking care of yourself and enjoying life, but you need to keep a balance so your time with God is not affected.

Some of us tend to give God things instead of spending time with Him, and we wonder why the enemy is attacking on every side. Our children are killing each other while we look on helplessly. Our homes are being destroyed, and we look on helplessly. The devil has stepped in with issues of your past to trap and hold you down, and you have fallen for his lies, but now is the time to change things. Now is the time to say 'enough is enough' and rise up for the battle. It is never too late. You cannot allow circumstances to dictate your future. Take back whatever the devil has stolen from you. Wipe your tears and wage war—war for your sanity, war for your dignity, war for the double God promised for your shame. Diagnose the problem, and take it to God in prayer.

As you get busy with your daily schedule, the enemy systematically gains ground. As you linger long at the debate table over which dress to wear or which color nail polish to use, the enemy gradually gains ground, dispersing his virus and demon spirits into your camp.

As you know, praying doesn't always bring a sudden and automatic disappearance of problems or overnight miracles. You have been around long enough to know that storms come into everybody's life. Whether you prepare for them or not, they are a part of our lives that we have to deal with.

A praying woman is a woman who is able to withstand and survive the storms of life because when they come, they find her connected strongly to God. The praying woman changes the spiritual climate in her life—her home, family, community, church, and nation. Yes, men are the spiritual heads, but prayer that avails much is not limited to gender but is given to all to profit society as a whole.

The praying woman's knowledge of the future enables her to create a strategy and establish a plan to combat the enemy's attack. An army that goes to war without a strategy is bound to lose. What will happen when the viral infection of deceit, anger, rage, self-pity, and low self-esteem attack you with voracious appetites for works of the flesh?

Will you let the controlling powers of anger, bitterness, and backbiting hold you in bondage? Will promiscuity and sexual addiction, impulsive shopping, and thoughts of revenge be your way of escape? Watch out! The devil is after you. He is after your husband, your children, your home, your finances, your self-esteem, your joy, your peace, and your health. He has been since Adam and Eve ate the apple in the Garden. It is a hate relationship. God has placed enmity between you and the devil, and he is out to destroy you. So wake up and face him. Your position is an important one. Remember, your seed destroyed the work of the devil on Calvary.

Chapter Three:

Deceptive Symptoms In Our Camp

Wake up from your sleep! Wake up from your slumber! The alarm shrieks just as it did in the era of Adam and Eve when the enemy entered the Garden to take what the Father had given them—their domain and sphere of influence. Be alert, for your adversary, the devil, is going about like a roaring lion, seeking whom he may devour. He is aware that a praying woman will not succumb easily to his lies, so he roams to and fro seeking one who is vulnerable and out of rank, one who has made prayer a five-minute affair.

Just what is this evil that seeks to control your life? It is described in Ephesians 6:12: "For we wrestle not against flesh and blood, but against principalities, against powers, against the rulers of the darkness of this world, against spiritual wickedness in high places."

Principalities are princes of the underworld who manipulate certain sections of the universe. Based on Daniel chapter 10, they are ruling spirits assigned over nations and cities. These spirits function by exerting their influence over heads of nations and kings. They seek to control the political lives of these nations, using the human heads as their main device of operation. Principalities are the highest of the rankings in the enemy's domain.

Powers are the second level of authority in the devil's domain. They exercise their authority over the decision-making bodies of a nation, influencing the structures of the governing authorities, encouraging wickedness by promoting injustice, and controlling lawmakers and policy-makers in places of authority. In Daniel 6:3, 6-8, the counselors and governors conspired against Daniel and got King Darius to issue decrees banning all religious activities. This same spirit is ruling today, banning prayer in schools and much more. It may be beneficial to take time to study the book of Daniel.

Powers also can sway the thoughts and feelings of average people. They can influence people to kill, to steal, and to indulge in all kinds of destructive behavior. These powers seek to control the mind and trap you in a web of deception. They have the power and ability to draw Christians away from praying as much as they should, to minimize their compassion and concern for lost souls, and so on. These powers also operate through the media. Their assignment is to make you believe a lie.

Rulers of darkness, as stated in Ephesians 6:12, is derived from the Greek *kosmokrateros*, which also means world rulers. These powers are mandated by the devil to promote false religion and occult practices, thereby enslaving the souls of men again in deception. These rulers of darkness aim to control. They will control anything they can lay their vile hands on. They deceive by false teachings, visions, and dreams. They promote horoscope, hypnotism, witchcraft, black and white magic, and much more.

The next is spiritual wickedness. The assignment of this wickedness is to promote lawlessness and wickedness in the land, ensnaring souls of men into all sorts of abominable sins, such as homosexuality, rape, lust, lasciviousness, suicide, and drug addiction. They are a well-organized cartel of evil, and you cannot afford to put on party gear. You are in a war so do not take anything for granted. The god of this world is working overtime, and you need to rise up and be in rank. You are wrestling with unseen beings without bodies. You are warring against powers of this world and against spiritual wickedness. Wicked spirits are foul and malicious and operate without mercy. They destroy anything good, and if they can, they will destroy you and what is dear to your heart in no time. The devil will strike anything, anytime, and anywhere that will hurt you the most.

So woman of God, lift yourself up, get yourself out of your state of slumber, put on your armor, and take the battle to the enemy's gate. When things go wrong in your life—at home, at church, in your marriage—don't look on aloof, but grab your weapon of warfare and begin to fight. The devil builds a web of deceit to fence you in. After the PWC virus attacks your mind-set, it begins to break your defenses. It moves in quickly with a strong barrage of works of the flesh: envy, jealousy, greed, pride, anger, the lust of the flesh and of the eyes—all of which are killers of the soul. As women, you have to fight these soul-killers daily. If you are honest enough, you agree with me. Women tend to be more emotional than men, thereby making women more susceptible to the works of the flesh that come through emotions.

Pride and anger are easy ways for the enemy to come into your life. Pride is a type of self-centeredness. Anytime you have allowed your pride to get in the way, all the works of the flesh weren't far off. Pride, when left alone, can draw you into areas that you never imagined were possible. Attitudes such as self-righteousness and un-forgiveness are companions of pride. You may think, "If I am right why should I forgive?" Or, you stepped on my toes, and I'm angry. I will destroy you. I will repay you for hurting me. These thoughts stem from a heart of pride.

If you have fallen into any of these works of the flesh, the devil has trapped you right where he wants you, and you've fallen for it. It is important to start praying before he uses these attitudes to destroy you. Don't let the devil use you to destroy you. Build your foundation on the Rock, Christ Jesus Himself, because if it is built on anything else, it is sure to crumble.

The devil probably gloats over the fact that great Christian music, eloquent speech, and enticing words of man's wisdom have replaced the power that comes through prayer. In today's society, pastors and Christians leaders know exactly which buttons to push to get results. They forget about whether they go about it God's way. Most men and women of God have acquired the Saul spirit. They are terrified of the people, so they give the people what they want—not what they need. It goes something like this: "If music is what you want, we have it in our church. If it's the message of prosperity, there's plenty of it. There's healing, too, and you can buy it in a prayer cloth. Whatever is convenient for you, we will accommodate. You don't have to pray anymore. Just call the prayer line, and someone will pray for you."

Is it wrong to ask for prayer assistance by calling a prayer line? No. But when all is said and done, and you are all alone facing the greatest giant that ever attacked your life, you should know exactly how to fight back with the Word of God. Don't fall for the easy way, for the easy way is no way at all.

Unfortunately, compromise in our churches today is strong. They say, "The millennium church is here for your convenience. Just come every Sunday, fill our seats, pay your tithe, provide us with what we need, and we will provide you with what you want. If you don't want to come to church on Sunday, just send in your tithe and offering. For your convenience, you can join us on www.millenniumchurch.com Why is there so much compromise? We are to set the standard for the world, not adopt its ways. We are to be emulated, and not to mimic what is wrong. According to God's word we should turn away from "Having a form of godliness, but denying the power thereof" (2 Timothy 3:5). We must make prayer a priority in our lives, or we will be in trouble.

We have replaced the real power of God with sensationalism, hype, and gimmicks. We know how to do the alleluia step and dance to the fast tempo of drums. We know how to spin around and shout at just the right time. We have trained a generation that cannot do exploits for God because they don't know Him. They don't know Him because they have not spent enough time with Him. They don't recognize His voice because they haven't listened to Him enough. This generation doesn't know anything about spending time in prayer. People in this generation lack the zeal to touch heaven and have heaven touch them in response.

There is a rising generation that doesn't know how to pray or wait on God; to lie before the porch and altar, weeping until deliverance comes. We are too composed and too stubborn to bend our knees in prayer. We have passed the job onto the mothers. Thank God for the old mothers of the church whose prayers have sustained some of us until now, but calling on Heaven is an individual responsibility.

I remember when I got saved a few decades ago and would go into the woods and the mountains to fast, pray, and wait on God. We learned then how to stay before God in travailing prayer. Those were moments and days that propelled us into our destiny, but today, we have assigned prophets in the church whose job it is to pray, seek God, and bring a word of prophesy for direction. We have put so much pressure on these poor souls to speak a prophetic word, whether God is speaking or not.

A true prophetic ministry is a praying ministry. How can you buy into the mind of God if you don't pray? Women need to be more cautious when submitting themselves to these prophetic gifts in the body today. There are truly gifted prophets who have learned what it means to submit in a local church and what it means to pray through the promises of God. They live a life of prayer and fasting, a life truly dedicated to God. However, we have placed our prophets in danger by substituting their voices for the voice of God. God speaks to us. God still speaks to His sheep, and His sheep know His voice. "My sheep hear my voice, and I know them, and they follow me" (John 10:27).

Just because you are prospering without prayer doesn't mean you are doing the right thing. The devil also can bring prosperity your way. A perfect example is when Jesus was tempted after His forty-day fast. The devil made a deal with Him that if Jesus would worship him, he would give Him the kingdom, as far as the eyes could see.

> *"Again, the devil taketh him up into an exceeding high mountain, and sheweth him all the kingdoms of the world, and the glory of them; and saith unto him, 'All these things will I give thee, if thou wilt fall down and worship me.' Then saith Jesus unto him, 'get thee hence, Satan: for it is written, Thou shalt worship the Lord thy God, and him only shalt thou serve'"* (Matthew 4:8-10).

As these verses illustrate, prosperity is not a sign of spirituality or maturity. This is where many Christians get stuck. Today the devil is still making deals. The devil is asking you to substitute God's way with your way. When the Spirit of God is upon a man or a woman, everyone can see it. When the power of God departs, it leaves so silently that you may not know it. Such was the case with Samson. When Samson lost his power through the deception of Delilah, he did not know the power had departed. "And he awoke out of his sleep, and said, 'I will go out as at other times before, and shake myself.' And he [knew] not that the LORD was departed from him" (Judges 16:20). Sad, isn't it?

His power was so evident that all could see it, yet when the power departed, it was so subtle that even he didn't know. Prosperity does not necessarily mean that you are in the will of God, especially if you are not fulfilling the principles of God's word. It is scary to see what happens when the Spirit of God departs from a person because God's spirit will not always strive with man. There comes a time when He takes leave, and all we are left with is plush organization and only the form of Godliness.

He's Got You Covered
While your battle started the day you gave your life to Christ, that day you also enlisted in God's army. This army is guaranteed to win, if it fights according to the Master's battle plan, which is laid out in His Word.

> *"Wherefore take unto you the whole armor of God that ye may be able to withstand in the evil day, and having done all, to stand. Stand therefore, having your loins girt about with truth, and having on the breastplate of righteousness; and your feet shod with the preparation of the gospel of peace; above all, taking the shield of faith, wherewith ye shall be able to quench all the fiery darts of the wicked. And the helmet of salvation, and the sword of the Spirit, which is the Word of God: praying always with all prayer and supplication in the Spirit, and watching thereunto with all perseverance and supplication for all saints."* Ephesians 6:13-18

How can you fight personalities without bodies, whom you cannot see? If you think about it, you almost want to give up, but don't. We are fighting according to the Word of God, which never fails and states that we have already won the battle. In addition, God has provided for us a spiritual armor. This armor is invisible to the natural eye, but effective in the spirit realm. The armor is a shroud of defense; the helmet, the breastplate, the shield of faith and the belt of truth, all are needed for self-defense in this battle.

Weapons of Defense

Gird your loins about with truth. This means walk in truthfulness, transparent to God and yourself. It is simply the absence of two-facedness and pretense. The purpose of a belt is to hold in place your clothing, thus the truth serves as the base that holds up your armor.

Wear a breastplate of righteousness. The word *righteousness* means *right standing with God*. This kind of righteousness is not acquired; it is imputed to you by the only righteous One, God Himself, through the blood of Jesus. There is nothing we can do in our own strength that can make us righteous, for Isaiah 64:6 states that our righteousness is like filthy rags before God. We can only stand in righteousness if we come through the blood of Jesus.

In our physical bodies, the breastplate covers the chest. Embedded in the chest are some of the most vital organs of the human body, including the heart and lungs. Proverbs 4:23 states, "Above all else, guard your heart, for it is the wellspring of life." We have an awesome responsibility to keep our hearts intact in the spirit, and in the natural.

It is also important to shod your feet with the preparation of the gospel of peace. This means put on shoes that are able to send you off with speed, preaching the Good News. It means to be eager to preach the gospel at all times, in all places, to all men. It means, woman of God, wear your boots for battle. Be prepared; don't be taken unaware.

The shield of faith helps us keep the fiery darts of the enemy at bay. Our faith is our unreserved confidence in God. It is complete reliance on the truth and integrity of God's Word. Fiery darts are flame-tipped arrows, a barrage of which is released before an assault. They are designed to weaken your defenses. Faith comes by hearing the Word of God. Build your faith in the Word. You need to eat the

Word daily and exercise your faith. Remember, without faith it is impossible to please God.

The helmet of salvation also provides protection. You know how important the head is. God in His sovereign wisdom encased the human head in a shell called the skull. The head contains the brain, the very organ of reason, which processes information. The head controls every other part of the body. If your head tells your hand to move, movement occurs. Proverbs 23:7 says as a man thinks in his heart so is he. The heart and the mind have a special connection. They work with each other. What controls your mind will influence your heart and ultimately control your life.

The helmet of salvation is designed to protect our minds and our whole perspective toward our Christian faith and life. Evil thoughts and imaginations are first conceived in the mind. To put your helmet on is to constantly read, study, and meditate on the Word of God. To meditate is to ponder, mutter, and reflect on the Word. This means the constant renewal of your thought patterns and mind settings by the Word of God—not meditation as in the eastern religions, which draws a blank that opens one's mind up to demonic control.

Weapons of Offense

Fortunately, apart from having several weapons of defense, we also have one weapon of offense: the sword of the Spirit, or the Word of God. With this weapon in hand, we need nothing else. This weapon contains the keys to defeat each move of the enemy. It is said that the best form of defense is to attack. But we can't fight this war with our own strength. We need the strength of the Spirit of God in the Word. The Holy Spirit knows and understands all things. He is the teacher, the One who leads us into all truth. When the devil came against Jesus after His forty-day fast, He fought back with the sword of the Spirit. Jesus was the Word, yet He prayed and fought with the Word. If He prayed the Word, what excuse do we have to rely on our own strength in prayer?

He needs you and me to take up His Word and make it our armor and shield. He is the shade upon our right hand. He covers the area that the shield leaves bare (the shield is usually held in the left hand, leaving the right side of a person bare). Ephesians 6:13 commands us to be equipped not with a physical or visible armor, but with the armor of the Word so we can withstand in the evil day, and having done all, to stand. This is just confirmation that evil and storms come to all of us, although my evil day may differ from yours.

The difference between a praying woman and a prayerless woman is that one survives the evil day, while the other is blown away by the storm. Watch the life of a woman who prays. Regardless of how low she falls, she always bounces back. Her tenacity goes way beyond her own strength. She may lose all her goods, but she's about to rock the world with a new class of goods. She may lose her family as did Job, but her persistence will bring yet another promise of God to fruition.

Inner strength does not merely come because you memorize a Scripture verse and chant it all day long. Inner strength is a result of time spent with God in prayer. In prayer, He breathes into you a fresh breath of life and inspiration that injects into you a tenacious and audacious power to live and move in perfect stride regardless of the situation or circumstances. This is where we as praying Christians differ from the world; the rest of the world watches in awe as we continue in peace and joy regardless of imminent danger and dire circumstances. It's comforting to know you can have this if you stand against the enemy in prayer.

Chapter Four:

Has the Devil Located You?

If you are not yet at a point where you feel peace and joy in all circumstances and you are bugged with the virus of prayerlessness, perhaps it is an indication that the devil has located and detected your weakness. There is an antidote. This powerful antidote works without fail. It is praying in other tongues. It is indeed a powerful tool in the hands of the believer.

I have experienced the joys of speaking in tongues. I have enjoyed the power imbedded in speaking in tongues and a life of consistent prayer because of this gift. Therefore, I encourage you to grab hold of it if you don't have it and use it if you do.

Ephesians 6:18 instructs us to pray always: "Praying always with all prayer and supplication in the Spirit, and watching thereunto with all perseverance and supplication for all saints."

You may say, "Oh, it's impossible to pray always," but Ephesians 6:18 states, "Praying always with all prayer and supplication in the Spirit, and watching thereunto with all perseverance and supplication for all saints." It is possible to pray without ceasing. It is sometimes hard for us to pray always because we go to God in our own strength, praying in our own capacity. There is an easier way to pray, and that is praying in the Holy Ghost, or praying in tongues. Prayer is difficult because it is a spiritual act and cannot be done in the flesh if one is to do it constantly.

Jude 1:20 talks about praying in the Spirit: "But ye, beloved, building up yourselves on your most holy faith, praying in the Holy Ghost."

However, praying in the Spirit does not appeal to our senses because it sounds silly and it puts us in a vulnerable position of not knowing what we are praying about. We would simply be saying, "I have no clue. I don't know what to say to You, Lord, and I feel silly just standing here blabbing on about what I can't understand." Guess what: That is exactly where God wants you. He wants you to totally depend on and trust in Him and His Word. Prayer generates total dependence upon God.

Praying in the Spirit is for your benefit. That's because the devil doesn't know entirely what God has planned for us or what our innermost desires and thoughts are until we speak them. Speaking in our understanding therefore gives the enemy an idea where we are and what we desire. With such information in his hand, he is able to cause delays and roadblocks. When we pray in the Spirit, we are praying the will and the mysteries of God, which neither the devil nor we can understand.

Speaking in unknown tongues gives you the upper hand, as stated in the Bible.

> *And he that searcheth the heart knoweth what is the mind of the Spirit, because he maketh intercession for the saints according to the will of God* (Romans 8:27).

> *For he that speaketh in an unknown tongue speaketh not unto men, but unto God: for no man understand him; howbeit in the spirit he maketh mysteries* (1 Corinthians 14:2).

By speaking in tongues, you don't only pray the will and the mysteries of God. You also confuse the devil. How is he going to launch an attack if he is not sure in which direction God is taking you? It is for this reason that he frustrates your prayer life. As long as you can stay in prayer, praying the mysteries of God, he loses. No wonder when you begin to pray, all kinds of things come up unexpectedly to steer you off course. The phone rings. A girlfriend you have not spoken to in six years suddenly found your number. A quick call to say hello becomes an hour-long conversation in an effort to catch up. Maybe your cell phone rings. Or you abruptly remember something you left incomplete in the office. The list goes on.

When things such as these happen, your efforts to pray are being hindered by the enemy attacking your mind. You will find your mind is a weapon of distraction as you pray, but you can beat this by praying in the Spirit.

Another benefit of praying in the Spirit is you pray the will of God. When I am not sure what the will of God is in any situation, I simply pray in tongues and allow time to unfold the mystery of His will. The will of God for your life is securely imbedded in your prayer language. When you pray in tongues, you go past reasoning, arguments of the mind, and spiritual roadblocks. Praying in tongues elevates you to the fast track. So while others are standing in line arguing out their petitions, you have gained easy access. When you pray in tongues, you pray selflessly and tap into the unlimited resources of God.

As you pray in tongues, you become an instrument and tool in the hands of the Holy Ghost. When you pray in tongues, you place yourself in a position where the Holy Ghost can use you to pray for continents, cities, communities, and churches. You may be praying for a pregnant woman in crisis, a flying aircraft, a captain at the mercies of the elements of the sea, someone wrongfully accused in court, or someone in imminent danger. Our scope of influence when we pray in the Holy Ghost is limitless. Prayers offered in tongues travel faster than the speed of light and accomplish much.

You may ask, "How do I speak in another tongue? What do I do to begin this walk in the Spirit?" Here are some scriptures to help:

And these signs will follow those who believe: in My name they will cast out demons; they will speak with new tongues (Mark 16:17 NKJV).

According to this Scripture, tongues are one of the signs that follow the believer. It is not to be rejected but to be embraced. It is a God-given tool that will help you on your Christian journey.

> *And they were filled with the Holy Spirit and began to speak with other tongues, as the Spirit gave them utterance* (Acts 2:4 NKJV).

This shows that speaking in tongues is not an effort of the mind, but it is given by the assistance of the Holy Spirit dwelling in someone.

> *And when Paul laid his hands upon them, the Holy Ghost came on them; and they spake with tongues, and prophesied* (Acts 19:6).

The laying on of hands is one way to receive the gifts of the Holy Ghost. They also are received by impartation or simply by asking God for them. A good example of the latter is the story of a young minister who trained in my church. She was brought up a staunch Catholic but later gave her life to Christ. At seventeen years old, she joined my church and was concerned about speaking in tongues. She felt it was silly and although she embraced most of the teachings, she could not accept the concept of speaking in tongues.

In all-night prayer meetings, which are a way of life for most of our churches in Africa, she would get frustrated because she covered the prayer topics in less than ten minutes. She did not enjoy praying all night, though she wanted to. However, she observed that those who prayed in tongues could go on for hours. In her frustration, she went into her prayer closet and asked God to give her the gift of the Spirit, if it was really from Him and of Him.

Days turned into weeks, and nothing happened. Then one day, as she was praying at home, she began to speak in tongues. It was so exhilarating that she could not stop. To keep her Catholic parents, who thought it was madness to speak in tongues, from noticing this gift, she ran into the bathroom and stayed there as long as she could, speaking in tongues. If her parents had heard her, a trip to the psychiatrist would have been inevitable.

Since then, more than sixteen years have passed, and she has grown into one of the strongest prayer warriors I know. She also walks in a powerful gift of praise and worship. I don't think it is a coincidence that she walks in the power that she walks in ministry. And it started simply by her asking God for this gift. Prayer is a power-producer and strength-builder. We do not pray because we seek power, we pray to seek His face.

Mighty woman, we need to pray always. We must pray when we feel like it as well as when we don't. We must pray when an immediate answer follows, and we still must pray when it feels as though God is on vacation. We need to pray when we think we know the solution to the problem and when we can't find any answers. We must pray when all is well and our children are flourishing like tender olive plants in our courts, and we must pray when our children have gone wayward. We need to pray not only when our husbands confess their undying love for us, but also when they walk out on us. We must pray when business is good and we have our money stacked away for a rainy day, and we must pray when we are neck high in debt. We pray with tears in our eyes and drops of sweat on our eyebrows. We pray when our hearts are bursting with unspeakable joy. There should be no convenient time to pray. We simply ought to pray always.

Praying daily means walking daily in His mercies. Mercy means exemption from judgment. Therefore, we need to free our minds daily from the guilt and mistakes of the past. The mercies of God give us confidence to approach His throne daily. The blood of Jesus confirms God's mercy, cleans us up, and infuses us with boldness and renewed self-assurance as we go before Him in prayer. There is no other way to approach Him except by His blood.

God releases to us fresh mercies each morning, according to His Word. "It is of the Lord's mercies that we are not consumed, because His compassions fail not. They are new every morning: great is thy faithfulness" (Lamentations 3:22-23). However, we must go to Him daily to receive these mercies. How else can we walk consistently in the mercies of God? Today's mercies may not cover tomorrow's sins. You need a constant renewal of His mercy.

The mercies of God can be compared to the manna that He provided to the children of Israel in Exodus.

> *This is what the LORD has commanded, 'Gather of it every man as much as he should eat; you shall take an omer apiece according to the number of persons each of you has in his tent.' The sons of Israel did so, and (some) gathered much and (some) little. When they measured it with an omer, he who had gathered much had no excess, and he who gathered little had no lack; every man gathered as much as he should eat. Moses said to them, 'Let no man leave any of it until morning.' But they did not listen to Moses, and some left part of it until morning, and it bred worms and became foul; and Moses was angry with them. They gathered it morning by morning, every man as much as he should eat; but when the sun grew hot, it would melt.* Exodus 16:16-21 NAS

He promised the men fresh manna each day, yet some of them felt they had to hold on to some until morning. Isn't that just like us? We pray today and think our prayer is enough to take us through the week. Then there are those who think they don't need the mercy of God. The self-righteous man thinks his works are sustaining him. We need to trust that upon the wings of each dawn, come the fresh mercy of God. Those who rise up early to seek it shall find it.

Just as when the men tried to save leftovers for the next day and they bred worms, if you are living off yesterday's mercy, you are living off the worms of the past. But when you let go of the past, you also let go of its challenges, pains, sins, iniquities, and transgressions. God does not remember yesterday's failures, but instead, He places them in the sea of forgetfulness and extends His mercy yet again. In other words, He was telling the children of Israel that He is more than enough to provide for each day. Like the children of Israel, you don't have to save leftovers. His mercies are new every morning.

Jesus encouraged His disciples to pray always and not faint: "Men ought always to pray, and not to faint" (Luke 18:1). Hold on to the horns of the altar; you can't afford to faint. There is an ingredient in prayer that is so imperative if we are to receive answers to our prayers. This ingredient is an obstinate adamancy to stay in consistent and prevalent prayer without wavering. This can be challenging, which is why Jesus encouraged us not to faint. He Himself was a praying man and understood the challenges that can occur as one embarks on a lifestyle of prayer. Prayer is hard work. Prayer drains you naturally but renews you spiritually. It is not easy to cultivate a lifestyle of prayer, but it is worth the effort.

Remember, your adversary will do anything and everything in his power to discourage you. He will persuade you that God is not interested in your prayers. But hang in there. God is not only interested, He sends His Holy Spirit to pray with you and through you with groanings which cannot be uttered (praying in tongues), leaving the devil confused about what is going on.

There are moments in life when fainting is such a comforting thought because we are weary inside and out from consistent prayers. We get so discouraged we could fly on the wings of anything that suggest that we faint just a little.

But you've got to wake up. The alarm is off, and the battle is fierce. You can't back down or back out. Don't break rank, and don't throw off your armor. Don't show up on the battlefield half dressed, without your helmet. And please take off your high-heeled shoes; they are not meant for battle. Instead, shod your feet in the preparation of the gospel of peace. Learn how to use your weapons appropriately. Do not be afraid of the enemy exposing you. Come through the victorious power of the blood of Jesus, and fight a good fight, mixing your warfare with faith.

The armor is for defense, and your sword is for offense. Don't cover hide the sword behind your back because the sword is meant for fighting. The Bible never said anything about your back being covered because you're not meant to turn your back in this battle. You are to face your enemy face on and win the good fight of faith.

Are you alert yet? There is deception out there, replacing prayer with human strategy, organization, and systems. It is common in the way many women manipulate and use their emotions as a tool for blackmail to get what they want. They know exactly how to wear their blouses low enough and their skirts high enough to get the attention they desire. They are using their God-given beauty for self-gain. They know how to sigh, cry, and frown to get their partners to give them what they want.

I can't stress enough the need for proper balance. I love organization and all the administrative structures put in place by my staff. While sometimes these things can eliminate people's need for God, underneath the organization and structure in my ministry are men and women praying round the clock. In fact, the ministry was founded on prayer. We learned early to connect to our Source, the Founder, and the Rock from whence we were hewn. This has made a tremendous difference in my life.

After more than twenty-five years in ministry, I cannot begin to tell you the storms that I've had to go through personally and the traumas these storms have brought. The one hundred-plus affiliate churches and branches I oversee have all gone through storms, but prayer has kept the weakened knots together. We have been through character assassinations, adverse media exposure, and other storms too many to number, but we are still prevailing by the cords that bind us strongly to our Source. I find strength to carry on daily, bearing my cross in prayer as I trudge on this pathway of destiny to fulfill God's mandate for my life.

Because I've been there, I understand where you may find yourself now, but you cannot afford to give up. Women face complex issues, issues too deep to vocalize and too personal to share. Some of you have gone through traumas that shook and disorganized your life. You may have been raped or emotionally abused, had an abortion, or faced some kind of rejection. For some of you, it is a broken relationship that was supposed to last. You gave your all and sacrificed a lot, and at the end of the day, you were left with broken promises, deep anguish, and diverse forms of rejection. Your life is now tarnished with a fear of relationships, a lack of trust, and many other emotional disorders.

The good news is that through intense and purposeful prayer, you can change your situation. You can once again enjoy your life and prepare for your future in God. While no emotional pain is easy to bear and emotions don't make sense, you can receive emotional stability through the Word of God and prayer.

There is an old hymn that says, "What a friend we have in Jesus, all our sins and greaves to bear, what a privilege to carry everything to God in prayer." You need to make Jesus your friend. You need to get off the phone and stop telling your friends about your problems. They cannot change them, nor can any man do for you what only God can do. The complexity of your problem is not so unique that God cannot handle it. Remember, all power in heaven and on earth belongs to the Lord. He can help you, and His hands are stretched out, waiting for you to come to Him in prayer.

Some women are accustomed to hiding behind the façade of a cute dress, makeup, and exhibiting false strength when they need help. But help can be obtained only when we go down on our knees and ask for it. We need to set our priorities straight by putting God first. We cannot build a house for God in which He would never live because we never created an atmosphere to keep Him there. We may create an atmosphere for Him to visit through our praise and worship, but can God call your structure His home, where He can come and abide with you always? Your outward appearance is not as important as the inward woman. God desires to live in you and through you. He desires to commune with you daily and directly.

The same goes for the woman who is building a business, her home, or career in her own strength. She apparently doesn't need God until calamity strikes. Then prayer becomes all-important. Wake up! You need a fresh connection to your power base, for your strength is little. Your ability to make it with your charm or on the stock market is not security. Consider what will happen when your charm and beauty fail, and the plastic surgeon cannot help you. What will happen when the stock market in which you have put your trust begins to crumble?

> *Except the LORD build the house, they labor in vain that build it, except the Lord keep the city, the watchman wakes but in vain* (Psalm 127:1).

As Christian women, we should be clear about who our source is. For some of you, your husband is your direct source, and he provides all you need. But there are some low points in your life where your husband cannot reach down and help. There are the multifaceted issues that no one can understand or help you with but God. There are single women who think marriage would solve all their problems, but marriage has challenges of its own. God must be your source. Prayer has a way of rearranging your thinking to the fact that if God doesn't handle it, no one can. Prayer is taking your eyes off yourself, your circumstances, and your social status, and looking unto God in humility and total dependence. We need to acknowledge and put God in the proper place in our lives. He is the priority, nothing else. Confuse your priority, and you mess up your structure.

There is a master builder who is willing to work with you until you fulfill your purpose. He will not force you to rely on Him, but He is encouraging you to do so.

Chapter Five:

The Pride of Life

Unfortunately, pride may be in our way. It may be keeping us from total dependence on God.

Pride could be what is keeping us from bowing down on our knees and admitting our need for God. We need God, not only for the weighty decisions in our personal and professional lives, but also for the ostensibly small ones.

The Bible says we should swallow our pride, and then He will provide healing. "If my people, which are called by my name, shall humble themselves and pray, and seek my face, and turn from their wicked ways; then will I hear from heaven, and will forgive their sin, and will heal their land" (2 Chronicles 7:14).

"If my people . . . shall humble themselves." The opposite of *humble* is arrogance, and a synonym for arrogance is pride. God is saying: "Here is the deal. You are my people, and you are called by no other name but mine. I'll make a deal with you: if you can humble yourself and pray [watch the progression], and seek my face, and turn from your wicked ways, I will forgive you and heal your land."

Your land may be your home, your relationship, your children, your church, your business, and so on. God is saying, "I see your struggle, and I want to reach out and help you, but you haven't stopped to invite Me. You're acting like you have it all under control, but daughter, I feel your need tugging at Me. But I see pride also. You're unable to ask for help. I know exactly where you are. I understand and have a solution and a plan for you. But can you just trust me?

"Take a moment, daughter, and let's be real. Take off the mask, shed the scales of falsehood, and let's have an honest conversation. I know that the sin of pride and stubbornness has kept us apart, but it's okay. Come, level with me now and seek my face. Search for me diligently. You know I cannot behold iniquity, so repent of your sins, and I will step right in and bring healing."

The toxin of pride and obstinacy in life is a killer. The sin of pride is abhorrent to God.

> *And he shall spread forth his hands in the midst of them, as he that swimmeth spreadeth forth his hands to swim: and he shall bring down their pride together with the spoils of their hands* (Isaiah 25:11).

> *And I will break the pride of your power; and I will make your heaven as iron, and your earth as brass* (Leviticus 26:19).

What is pride? Pride is self-importance and self-centeredness, an unduly high opinion of one's self-worth. Pride causes one to see the world only through his or her own eyes. Any other opinion is inferior to the prideful man. Pride says, "Look at me. I am high and lifted up. I don't need you. I have all I need, and that is myself."

Arrogance is knocking us off God's favor list. God can't stand conceit. It doesn't matter if it is the pride of a nation or the pride of an individual, God will make sure that pride comes down. History is proof. Think about what happened where man thought he was untouchable because of some creation of his own hand.

Consider the "unsinkable" *Titanic*. On April 14, 1912, nature tragically proved man wrong. Nature proved that the *Titanic* was sinkable. Our pride increases as our need for our Creator decreases, as the created says to the Creator, "I don't need you. I will do fine on my own."

"The wicked, through the pride of his countenance, will not seek after God: God is not in all his thoughts" (Psalm 10:4). However, the Creator is the One who has the blueprint. He knows exactly what His creation needs and when.

Just as cars need regular servicing or they will break down, and just as we need to eat regularly to survive, we need servicing from God on a daily basis to keep running smoothly. When we deny our need for God in our daily lives, we inevitably break down. God makes it His business to bring down the prideful person. Many young Christians miss it in life because they thought they had it together and didn't need God or anybody else. Some women are so adamant in their ways that nothing causes them to bow or bend.

Pride was first recorded when Lucifer thought it would be a really neat idea to be like God. He did not need God; his self-centeredness told him he could make it on his own, that he could be compared to God and thus he could usurp His throne. Lucifer had recognition, talent, a prestigious position, and beauty, which added up to power. The true character of a man or women shines through when he or she is placed in power. A proud person with power is like a bloodsucking leech on flesh—he just can't get enough. Seeming prosperity was soon to test Lucifer. The prestige went to his head, and he thought he was it. When this happens to people, it destroys them.

Proverbs 1:32 says, "For the turning away of the simple shall slay them, and the prosperity of fools shall destroy them."

If you want to test a person for pride, just place him or her in the midst of wealth. How does this person treat his or her parents, family, or peers? Many young men and women who come into prestige and prosperity will change adversely. Many try to buy and manipulate their way to the top, but the book of Psalms clearly says the promotion comes from God. While pride can be hidden safely in the life of a poor man or woman, prosperity exposes it.

We've been created with a perpetual need for our Creator. Pride will deny you the joys and comfort of God's guidance and leadership. The pride of life, coupled with stubbornness, is a self-destructive mechanism. It will place you in opposition to your Creator and in battle with yourself—neither of which you can win. In our Christian journey, pride is the quickest way of descent.

Nebuchadnezzar was a man filled with pride. He commanded kingdoms and nations and was a force and power to be reckoned with in his day. When his pride got in the way, he became an example for God to show us clearly and distinctively what pride can do to a man. God turned the high-mindedness of Nebuchadnezzar into foolishness and sent him on his way, mad. When God sees pride in the life of a person, He has only one option: to resist him until he realizes he is mere man. Note that the devil doesn't have anything to do with this; it is a God thing. The devil may lead you on the path to pride, but God puts in motion the wheels of descent into the reality of who is really in charge.

Here's Nebuchadnezzar's story:

"The king spake, and said is not this Babylon, that I have built for the house of the kingdom by the might of my power, and for the honor of my majesty? While the word was in the king's mouth, there fell a voice from heaven, saying, O king Nebuchadnezzar, to thee it is spoken; the kingdom is departed from thee. And they shall drive thee from men, and thy dwelling shall be with the beast of the field; they shall make thee to eat grass as an oxen, and his body was wet with the dew of heaven, till his hairs were grown like eagles' feathers, and his nails like birds' claws.

And at the end of the days I Nebuchadnezzar lifted up mine eyes unto heaven, and mind understanding returned to me, and I blessed the most High, and I praised and honored him that liveth forever, whose dominion is an everlasting dominion, and his kingdom is from generation to generation: And all the inhabitants of the earth are reputed as nothing: and he doeth according to his will in the army of heaven, and among the inhabitants of the earth: and none can say his hand, or say unto him, What doest thou? At the same time my reason returned to me; and for the glory of my kingdom, mine honor and brightness returned unto me; and my counselors and my lords sought unto me; and I was established in my kingdom, and excellent majesty was added unto me. Now I, Nebuchadnezzar, praise and extol and honor the King of heaven, all whose works are truth, and his ways judgment: and those that walk in pride he is able to abase." Daniel 4:30-37

This story can't be much clearer. And he lived to tell his own story. No one wrote it for him; he wrote it in his own words. He remembered the time when he went insane. He remembered the details of his insanity and his inability to restore himself. Can you imagine what torment that must have been—to be trapped in a barricade of insanity and yet have enough awareness to know you are losing it and have no power to control yourself? He ends with words of praise to the only wise and living God, who sits in the circles of the earth, and gives a factual word of caution that those who walk in pride: He is able to subjugate.

Because of the seriousness of this virus called pride and its best friend stubbornness, here are more related scriptures. Nothing or no one says it better than these proverbs on the consequences of pride.

Everyone that is proud in heart is an abomination to the Lord: though hand join in hand, he shall not be unpunished (Proverbs 16:5).

If I were to tell you that pride is an abomination, you would say I was taking things a bit too far. But the Bible says that clearly in that verse. Abomination is another word for atrocity, eyesore, hatred, and outrage. This is intense. Can you feel the heart of the Father toward pride? The antidote to breaking pride is prayer and fasting. *A greedy man stirs up dissension, but he who trusts in the LORD will prosper.* (Proverbs 28:25). New International Version.

Because pride wants its way always and is always right in its own eyes, it inevitably produces strife wherever it's found. No one is exempt from pride. It is subtle and can fall into the lap of anyone who is making progress in life. It can gradually eliminate your need for God, as sometimes systems and organizations can do.

For example, why ask God for money if you can use your credit card? Why obey Him when He says to pay off your house when you can get a thirty-year mortgage? Society, with all its great technology, is steering us away from the only sure foundation we have—God. As a woman, you have to work hard at killing pride and refusing stubbornness and rebellion. Don't forget that rebellion is like the sin of witchcraft. When you resist truth, you resist God Himself, for God is truth.

Society accepts pride, and almost expects it from us. Feminist groups tell us it's all right to fight for your rights, even if they contradict the Word of God. Get an abortion if you want; it is your right and your choice. But what about the rights and what the Bible says about the life of an unborn child? Some women these days are fighting for everything, and mostly for what is wrong in the eyes of God. This is not to say that women should be treated any way and should take whatever is dished out to them in a man's world. Women should be treated fairly and with much respect, but we need to be careful we don't draw the line in direct defiance of the Word of God. Pride would lead us to a fall. Placing yourself on your knees daily is a deterrent to pride. A woman on her knees is a woman in need of God. Honor and humility are as inseparable as pride and fall.

As the following two verses show, pride releases the wrath of the Lord, and humility releases His favor.

> *Pride goeth before destruction, and a haughty spirit before a fall"* (Proverbs 16:18).

> *A man's pride shall bring him low: but honor shall uphold the humble in spirit* (Proverbs 29:23).

It is indeed a fearful thing to fall into the hands of the Lord. I will opt for His mercy anytime.

Are you struggling with the act of prayer? Take a moment and check yourself. Maybe pride is separating you from God. Many times the anger of disappointment and dashed expectations have opened the door for the enemy to step in with a strong spirit of arrogance and self-reliance. Being independent as a woman is not such a bad thing—except when this independence draws you away from God.

Let's repent and move on to another level. Search your heart briefly before moving on to the next chapter. It would so release your heart and bring liberty to your soul.

Chapter Six:

Many Christians are Disillusioned

If not pride, you may have other attitudes keeping you from a healthy prayer life.

However, James 5:16 states the benefits of prayer, clearly and simply: "The effectual fervent prayer of a righteous man availed much."

Many Christians don't think prayer is for them. They think one must be gifted in the area of prayer or called specifically to a prayer ministry to pray consistently. That is simply not true. Prayer is for everyone.

Some people are of the attitude that if God is God, and He knows the end from the beginning and vice versa, then God will work things out in His own time. I have heard many Christians say, "God gave me a word of prophecy, and that settles it. I will just wait for it to come to pass." By just waiting, they never pray that word into fruition. They never remind God of this word of prophecy. They never war with the word of prophecy. They simply daydream about it.

What some people don't know is that you need to enforce God's prophetic word—just as a police officer enforces the law—and superimpose the victory into this realm. For example, the police officer ensures that the law is obeyed and carried out. The sight of an officer in uniform is enough to bring order to some chaotic situations. When he pulls out his badge, he confirms his authority, and when he pulls out his gun, he's telling you he's got the power.

Consider the prophetic word of God or His written Word, the law. We are His law-enforcing agents. He has given us His Son Jesus, the badge of authority, and His Word, representing the source of power. Take that Word and enforce it. Arrest every contrary spirit that seeks to steal, delay, or kill the Word of God. Don't forget, the devil comes to steal, kill, and destroy. You and the Word are his targets. God's antidote for our daily challenges is the call of God for us to pray always.

> *This charge I commit unto thee, son Timothy, according to the prophecies which went before on thee, that thou by them mightiest war a good warfare; holding faith, and a good conscience; which some having put away concerning faith have made shipwreck* (1 Timothy 1:18-19).

By this charge, Paul gave Timothy the keys whereby he would be able to secure God's purposes concerning his life and would not end up shipwrecked in the great spiritual battle raging in the heavenlies and on earth. He also made it clear that the manifestation of God's promises and prophecies would be brought about by warfare.

Years in ministry have brought to my attention the great deception from the forces of darkness. That deception is "that as long as God has given the promise of prophecy, it will come to pass, so just relax, sleep, and wait for the fulfillment". In hindsight, don't you realize that the greatest battles you ever faced in life came soon after a strong prophetic word from God? Maybe it was a *rhema* word God gave you in your personal time of fellowship, yet everything contrary to that word took place.

Apart from the written Word, the devil does not know God's exact purpose for your life in a particular area until God reveals it through prophecy. As soon as the devil and his troops hear this word of prophecy, they take measures in the realm of the spirit and in the realms of the natural to ensure it never comes to pass. When the devil fights the Word of God, things get worse before they get better. They only get better when we hang in there in faith. We doubt too quickly and give up too easily. We run from the battle in doubt and defeat. Remember Esther, a woman who was willing to believe God to step into a situation at the expense of her own life? Stop doubting the Word of God when things seem to be going the wrong way. It is just a demonic onslaught to take you off course. Stay on course. Don't give in to pain. Keep pushing and keep persisting until something breaks.

Ignorance of what the devil is doing will send you packing and walking away from your purpose. "Therefore my people are gone into captivity, because they have no knowledge" (Isaiah 5:13). Timothy had a nonchalant attitude toward the prophecies of God. Perhaps this bothered Paul, and that's why Paul, the same Paul who once killed believers, now saved by grace, told Timothy to war with the prophecies. Paul probably said to himself, "Timothy is too cool about this prophecy. He needs to wake up in prayer, or it will never come to pass." Perhaps he was too cool, too intact, and too composed to show any distress about the delay of the Word of God.

The devil throws a party when he comes into contact with an ignorant believer. He draws a circle around them because he lacks understanding of the principles of the kingdom and the rules of battle in the realm of the spirit. Maybe you're saying, "I haven't received any prophetic word from the Lord over my life." If this is the case, know that God has thousands of promises in the Bible waiting to be manifested in the lives of believers. Most don't come to pass because we don't want to pay the price to effect their manifestation.

However, Daniel saw the importance of persistent prayer, as shown in Daniel 10:1-14. In this account, Daniel is on a twenty-one-day fast, seeking some words from God pertaining to the things that would befall his people in the future. At the end of the third week, he was by the great river Hiddekel, known today in Iraq as the Tigris. By the banks of the river, he beheld the most terrible sight—that of an angel coming right out of the spiritual warfare with the ruling satanic prince over the Persian Empire. So savage had been the fight in the heavens over Persia that the angel is described as having a face that resembled lightning, eyes that blazed like lamps of fire, and arms and feet like colored brass. This shows how fierce battles in the spirit can be when we engage in combat with the forces of darkness.

For Daniel, the sight was so terrible to behold that he fainted. After his resuscitation, the angel gave him a crucial fact and revelation of what caused the delay of Daniel's answer to his prayer.

> *But the prince of the kingdom of Persia withstood me one and twenty days; but, lo Michael, one of the chief princes, came to help me; and I remained there with the kings of Persia* (Daniel 10:13).

On the way from heaven with an answer to prayer, the angel encountered the evil prince of Persia. A territorial principality that governed the whole Persian Empire interrupted the angel, trying to stop him from reaching Daniel with the message from God. Meanwhile, Daniel was on his face in persistent prayer. He did not give up the fight and take a nap. He was desperate enough to be consistent, simply obeying God's principle of praying without ceasing.

There is a reward that comes when one persists in prayer. "Lest Satan should get an advantage of us: for we are not ignorant of his devices" (2 Corinthians 2:11). Even though the victory already exists in the spirit, we release it into the natural realm by staying consistent in prayer. We win if we stick to the Word, the plan, and the way. It is by no means easy, but it's effective. Don't think for a moment that your prayers don't touch God because they do.

> *(For the weapons of our warfare are not carnal, but mighty through God to the pulling down of strong holds;) casting down imaginations, and every high thing that exalteth itself against the knowledge of God, and bringing into captivity every thought to the obedience of Christ* (2 Corinthians 10:4-5).

I have a few personal stories that prove there is power in prayer and constant communication with our Maker. The first example took place a few years ago. I was scheduled to be on a flight to a neighboring African country. Preparations had been made for my arrival and speaking engagements, and advertisements had gone out. But when it was time for me to travel, the Lord told me not to go on that flight. I reluctantly called and canceled. The flight I was supposed to be on ended up crashing.

Another time I was visiting one of my friends in the ministry in the Virgin Islands when CNN issued a tornado warning for the area. The pastor I was visiting was greatly disturbed. Of course, I was also concerned since I was there at the time. I asked the Lord what to do, and He told me to speak to the storm and command it to go back where it came from. I prayed, just as the Lord commanded. The storm kept approaching as we listened to updates, but when it hit the shores, it made a U-turn. Tell me prayer doesn't change things.

Years later, I visited the same island, and one night, the Lord woke me up and asked me to leave town immediately. It was almost midnight. I called the airlines to see if they had any flights departing, and was told there were no flights at that time of the night. Then I told my assistant with whom I was traveling to take a taxi to the airport and find us a flight out of there while I packed my things. He looked at me as though I were mad. He said there were no flights at that time of night. I told him simply to do as I had told him. He unenthusiastically did as I had asked. He called me later to confirm that there were no flights leaving town. I insisted he check again.

He called back a few minutes later and said an American Airlines flight scheduled to leave in the morning had decided to leave the island at about 1 A.M. We made it out of town only to find out that a storm hit not long after we left. As these stories prove, when we have a relationship with God, He speaks to us, and we recognize His voice because we are familiar with it.

Chapter Seven:

The Cure for PWC

If you have let pride get in the way, or if you have felt prayer is not for you, or if you have strayed from a lifestyle of persistent prayer for some other reason, there is still hope for your future. The remedy that worked in the past still cures Prayerlessness Without Ceasing. The cure for PWC is etched in the Word of God.

There are many accounts of people in the Bible who prayed through the promises of God. Elijah was one of them. He prayed that it would not rain for three-and-a-half years, and for that period, it did not rain. When he prayed again that it should rain, rain poured from heaven. "And he prayed again, and the heaven gave rain, and the earth brought forth her fruit" (James 5:18). Elijah's ability to persist in prayer makes him a man to imitate.

Daniel was also a man of consistent prayer. His prayers reached heaven, brought into manifestation the prophecies of God for a whole nation, and exalted God in a godless society. Daniel was bold in his beliefs. His prayers kept him secure in a society where serving God was a suicide attempt. He was willing to die for what he believed.

Then there is the story of David, whose relationship with God and whose prayers brought about the majority of the psalms. David's dependence on God can't be missed. David was a man of prayer, praise, and worship.

Moses was a man who interceded constantly for the people of Israel. He was a leader upon whom the people depended greatly. The pressure on Moses must have been daunting. He had the responsibility of leading a whole nation out of bondage without knowing the details of God's plan. He was aware that he could not lead the people of God except by the divine direction of God. Thus, he constantly asked God what to do next. Each day, he had to trust God's new direction for a murmuring people whose attitudes always led him back to his knees seeking God's face. His character and innate need for God awarded him the title "meekest man on earth." The one time pride got in the way, he missed seeing the Promised Land. (You can read the story of Moses, a remarkable man of God, in the book of Exodus.)

Abraham, father of many nations, was a man of faith and prayer. He held on to God's impossible promise until its manifestation. Today, you and I are heirs of that promise.

The praying men and women of the Bible enjoyed remarkable promises because of their relationship with God, based on prayer. Hannah changed her situation of childlessness through prayer. God blessed Deborah with the wisdom to judge a nation. Esther fasted and took a bold step to turn a whole nation around. These are only a few of many examples in the Bible.

Of all the examples, Cornelius' prayer life touches me most. He is simply introduced to us as "a certain man." The only identity we have for this man is that he was a centurion who belonged to an Italian band. This man has no genealogical background linking him to anyone or any group of people. However, he bypassed all those who had a favorable possibility of being mentioned in the Bible and secured himself a position there through his prayer life.

> *There was a certain man in Caesarea called Cornelius, a centurion of the band called the Italian band, a devout man, and one that feared God with all his house, which gave much alms to people, and prayed to God always. He saw in a vision evidently about the ninth hour of the day an angel of God coming in to him, and saying unto him, 'Cornelius.' And when he looked on him, he was afraid, and said, 'What is it,*

Lord?' And he said unto him, 'Thy prayers and thine alms are come up for a memorial before God. And now send men to Joppa, and call for one Simon, whose surname is Peter.' Acts 10:1-6

This scripture says Cornelius prayed always. His continuity touched the heart of God, and God had no choice but to intercept and send Him the help he needed.

Prayer breaks all limits. Men of prayer such as Job, Paul, and others who have achieved great accomplishments, were just like you and me.

A Solid Foundation

Prayer was the foundation of the early church. After the death of Jesus, the disciples continued with the work He had started. They had been with Jesus long enough to adopt His ways. They knew prayer was what saw Him through to the end. We find them praying together many times.

These all continued with one accord in prayer and supplication, with the women, and Mary the mother of Jesus, and with his brethren (Acts 1:14).

And they continued steadfastly in the apostles' doctrine and fellowship, and in breaking of bread, and in prayers (Acts 2:42).

Prayer brought unity, and unity produced the power of God.

The first church had balance. Though the people had their doctrines, they learned to balance them with prayer. Prayer was the basis for everything they did and decided.

Even Pentecost happened as a result of prayer.

And when they had prayed, the place was shaken where they were assembled together; and they were filled with the Holy Ghost, and they spake the Word of God with boldness (Acts 4:31).

There were many men of God who continued in prayer and encouraged the church to pray. Paul, the writer of most of the epistles, was one who had a consistent prayer life. He also encouraged the church to pray always.

Following are several scriptures about more of these men.

Be careful for nothing; but in everything by prayer and supplication with thanksgiving let your request be made known unto God (Philippians 4:6).

For this cause we also, since the day we heard it, do not cease to pray for you, and to desire that ye might be filled with the knowledge of his will in all wisdom and spiritual understanding (Colossians 1:9).

Continue in prayer, and watch in the same with thanksgiving (Colossians 4:2).

Withal praying also for us, that God would open unto us a door of utterance, to speak the mystery of Christ, for which I am also in bonds (Colossians 4:3).

We give thanks to God always for you all, making mention of you in our prayers (1 Thessalonians 1:2).

Night and day praying exceedingly that we might see your face, and might perfect that which is lacking in our faith (1 Thessalonians 3:10).

Now Peter and John went up together into the temple at the hour of prayer, being the ninth hour (Acts 3:1).

But we will give ourselves continually in prayer, and to the ministry of the Word (Acts 6:4).

Epaphras, who is one of you, a servant of Christ, saluteth you, always laboring fervently for you in prayer, that ye may stand perfect and complete in all the will of God (Colossians 4:12).

Pray without ceasing (1 Thessalonians 5:17).

Finally, brethren, pray for us, that the word of the Lord may have free course, and be glorified, even as it is with you (2 Thessalonians 3:1).

I exhort therefore, that, first of all, supplications, prayers, intercessions, and giving thanks, be made for all men (1 Timothy 2:1).

I will therefore that men pray everywhere, lifting up holy hands, without wrath and doubting (1 Timothy 2:8).

Is any among you afflicted? Let him pray. Is any merry? Let him sing psalms (James 5:13).

Peter therefore was kept in prison: but prayer was made without ceasing of the church unto God for him (Acts 12:5).

And when they had ordained them elders in every church, and had prayed with fasting, they commended them to the Lord, on whom they believed (Acts 14:23).

The early church lived a life of prayer. The people survived the times because they prayed. If the church of today is to survive the times, prayer has to take place—prayer for the nations, prayer for the communities, prayer for the saved, prayer for the unsaved, prayer for the sick, prayer for the afflicted, prayer for all saints, prayer for presidents and rulers of our world. Prayer is our call to duty.

However, you need to grow in prayer. Start by praying for yourself and building your way up to heavy-duty prayer. Study the Word and arm yourself with the power of the sword and take your position. There is power in prayer. There is deliverance in the prayers that you pray. Don't underestimate your power in prayer. Change the way you fight your battles. Change the atmosphere in your home and your business or ministry through prayer. Don't depend on your own strength but rather on the unquestionable power of prayer.

Chapter Eight:

The Ultimate Praying Man

Of all the great men of prayer, one stands out above the rest. He is a man I admire greatly and whose prayer life you should emulate. He lived a rather short life and had a short ministry, yet the impact He made is still felt in our world today. His life has transformed the hearts of many a stubborn man and woman and has delivered the captives from the prisons that once held them bound. Songs are still being sung about Him, and no force or power has been able to erase His name or His influence from the world.

This ultimate man of prayer is none other than Christ Jesus, our Lord. He performed many miracles and walked on water. He raised the dead and healed the sick. The Bible clearly says He was all man. He was subject to temptations, just as we are, and yet He was found without sin.

He was the Son of God, but He was just like you and me. We often don't think about the fact He experienced what we do when we face difficult situations. We look to other characters in the Bible (though there's nothing wrong with that) and dismiss Him as God. But remember, He was touched by the feelings of your infirmities. He understands and knows your weaknesses and your frailty. That is why He is forever making intercession for you. He felt what you feel. Remember Isaiah's account of Him? He was bruised for our iniquity. This man of prayer was wounded for our transgressions, and the chastisement of our peace was upon Him. This means He was reprimanded for your sins. He was a man of sorrows and was well acquainted with grief. He was despised and rejected. He understands what you are going through. As a man, Jesus was able to perform miracles because He prayed. He was securely connected. As a human, His only source of contacting the Father was through prayer. He often would retreat into the mountains alone to pray. And before every major decision or miracle, Jesus was away somewhere praying.

He Prayed Before Embarking on His Ministry

Before He stepped out into ministry, He fasted and prayed in the wilderness for forty days and nights. He didn't just wake up one day and say, "Hmmm. I feel good today. I'm excited about God, so let me start a ministry." Instead, He spent time before God, waiting, fasting, and praying.

He Prayed Before Selecting the Twelve Apostles

He prayed all night before choosing the apostles, as Luke 6:12-13 says: "And it came to pass in those days, that he went out into a mountain to pray, and continued all night in prayer to God. And when it was day, he called unto him his disciples: and of them he chose twelve, whom also he named apostles."

He could not choose the Twelve by sight. He had to choose them through the Father's eye, for each of these apostles had a purpose. Unlike Jesus, we seldom pray to God for guidance as we make major decisions about our business, marriage, and other choices that alter the course of our lives. We logically select a partner or carry on our business in the flesh. However, God is interested in everything we do. And with the right choices, we ultimately will fulfill God's will through us.

When we pray before our decisions, it not only helps us to fulfill our purpose, but that of others as well. Peter's purpose had to be fulfilled, but that would not have happened if Jesus had not sought the Father before making His choice. Therefore, if you are to succeed in life, you need to ask God to bring into your path people whose lives you can affect and people who can affect you as well so that in the end, the will of the Father will be fulfilled in your life and in theirs.

How do you protect your home and your children? How do you choose your workers? Do you just do what you think, or do you ask God's opinions?

Jesus Continued to Pray While in Ministry

While in ministry, He prayed to the Father many times in solitude.

> *And in the morning, rising up a great while before day, he went out and departed into a solitary place, and there prayed* (Mark 1:35).

> *And it came to pass, as he was alone praying, His disciples were with Him* (Luke 9:18).

The fewer interruptions and hindrances you have in prayer, the better the focus and intensity. Praying in the early hours of the morning when most of the world is sleeping is a way to reduce interruptions. Also, early in the morning, the mind is less taxed. I encourage you to find your own quiet time each day to spend with God. Great men of the recent past were able to obtain great victories through the avenue of persistent prayer. Take, for example, John Knox, Smith Wigglesworth, and Kathryn Kuhlman. These people made a great impact on their generation because they knew how to pray. Kathryn Kuhlman would get on her knees reverently each time before she went out to preach and bring God's power of healing to people.

Jesus' source of power can be directly traced to what He did in His quiet time. What do you do in your quiet time? Are you surfing the Internet, or are you seeking God's face? Are you looking at the statistics that always point to your limitations, or are you seeking your God of no limits?

Jesus' disciples wanted to learn to pray as He did. Don't you? "And it came to pass, that, as he was praying in a certain place, when he ceased, one of his disciples said unto him, 'Lord, teach us to pray, as John also taught his disciples'" (Luke 11:1).

Jesus Prayed before Major Miracles

Preceding most of Jesus' supernatural encounters, He prayed. Here is one example:

> *And when he had sent the multitudes away, he went up into a mountain apart to pray: and when the evening was come, he was there alone. But the ship was now in the midst of the sea, tossed with waves: for the wind was contrary. And in the fourth watch of the night Jesus went unto them, walking on the sea. And when the disciples saw him walking on the sea, they were troubled, saying, "It is a spirit"; and they cried out for fear* (Matthew 14:23-26).

Most of us think Jesus just decided to walk on water to prove a point—that He was the God-man. But His supernatural ability to walk on water occurred because of prayer. Jesus prayed until the fourth watch, and if a watch consists of three hours, it may be safe to assume that Jesus prayed for about twelve hours. This shows important prayer is, so please don't take it for granted.

Another example was when He had gone up the mountain to pray with three of His apostles. Luke says that as He prayed, His appearance changed.

> *He took Peter and John and James, and went up into the mountain to pray. And as he prayed, the fashion of his countenance was altered, and his raiment was white and glistering* (Luke 9:28-29).

Can you feel the power of prayer? Prayer places you outside the natural realm with its limitations and into a realm of impossibilities. Prayer coupled with faith is dynamite. It releases God's hand of miracles, signs, and wonders. Jesus assured us that if we talk in the ways of God, greater works than He did shall we do.

Jesus Prayed Himself through the Cross Experience

Perhaps the most touching and intense prayer time Jesus had was during the hours before His death, in the Garden of Gethsemane, as His flesh and spirit battled with the will of God. Here we see the frailty of the Messiah man. We witness His anguish as He re-evaluated death on the cross. He counted the cost and grief-stricken, pleaded for the cup to pass Him by.

> *Then cometh Jesus with them unto a place called Gethsemane, and saith unto the disciples, "Sit ye here, while I go and pray yonder." And he took with him Peter and the two sons of Zebedee, and began to be sorrowful and very heavy. Then saith he unto them, "My soul is exceedingly sorrowful, even unto death: Tarry ye here, and watch with me." And he went a little further, and fell on his face, and prayed, saying, "O my Father, if it be possible, let this cup pass from me: nevertheless not as I will, but as thou will"* (Matthew 26:36-39).

In these verses, we see Him weigh His deepest desire with the will of the Father. For a moment, He exercised His free will as a man (His right to choose), then recoiled into the shell of God's will. This is a price too great, a death too painful. Imagine His life flashing before Him—He had lived a life free of sin, which was not easy for a man to do. He had loved with all His heart, through rejection, false accusations, and threats of being stoned. He had paid a dear price every step of the way, and like a lamb led to the slaughter, He had not defended Himself, only His course to fulfill God's purpose. He must have thought, "Father, I am blameless. Why should I die for the sins of the world?"

As He continued to pray, He could feel the gradual separation from the Father as the sins of each person who ever lived and who would ever live on the face of the earth were laid on Him. In tremendous distress and apprehension, He went to check on His disciples, whom He had chosen to be with Him. Maybe they would offer a degree of comfort, a way to escape His lonely dilemma. Upon His arrival, they were all asleep.

Jesus was faced with the frailty of man. He encouraged them to pray, but out of His own experience, He offered a word of understanding that the spirit indeed is willing but the body is weak. He could identify with their weakness, for He felt it, too.

Watch and pray, that ye enter not into temptation: the spirit indeed is willing, but the flesh is weak (Matthew 26:41).

He made His way back to pray, sweat streaming down His face. He tried hopelessly to exercise His rights as a man, His right to choose yet again. He painfully prayed for God's will to be done. As the sense of separation from the Father lay heavily on His heart, sweat like blood dripped from His face, and he could sense the pressure of this mission. It was the reason He was sent; yet it was the hardest task yet. He knew He would not make it without the help of the Father. He knew the liberation of posterity; generations to come depended on the decision of the moment.

He went away again the second time, and prayed, saying, "O my Father, if this cup may not pass away from me, except I drink it, thy will be done" (Matthew 26:42).

Jesus didn't stop there. He prayed consistently and persistently, enforcing the will of the Father into manifestation. He was completely consumed by His communication with the Father. He knew He could not do it alone, and His humility drew Him time and again to His Father. Jesus didn't pray once or twice; He prayed the same prayer three times.

And he left them, and went away again, and prayed the third time, saying the same words (Matthew 26:44).

Sometimes the will of God is not easy. We need to enforce it in prayer until our spirit, soul, and body are in total alignment to His will.

Remember, even as Jesus prayed in the days of His flesh to be saved from premature death thereby aborting His mission, He, through, prayer prohibited the possible abortion of His mission.

Who in the days of His flesh, when he had offered up prayers and supplication with strong crying and tears unto him that was able to save him from death, and was heard in that he feared; though he were a Son, yet learned he obedience by the things which he suffered (Hebrews 5:7-8).

The plan of the enemy is to abort your vision. There is no substitute for prayer because it is a necessity in the life of the believer. Ultimately, the praying person survives, and Jesus is proof.

Jesus walked on water; He raised the dead, He opened blind eyes, He cast out devils and set captives free. He restored broken lives, fulfilling every iota of His ministry to the very end. Prayer was the secret to His success.

Prayer exalts God and conforms us to His will. Prayer superimposes the manifestation of the will of God into the natural realm. It is the breeding ground for signs, wonders, and miracles. Prayer protects us and releases God's glory in our lives.

Prayer is not everything, but prayer changes everything. It is the foundation that holds the building together. It is the core device that upholds the other equipment. It strengthens our relationship with God, and out of that relationship emanates love, faith, and everything else we need to complete us in our Christian walk.

It will break down the walls of racism and tear down the dividing walls of segregation. Prayer will enforce the will of God in your life. It will draw the backslider back to God. It will literally change ungodly legislation in a community. Prayer destroys the works of darkness and breaks its power of operation. Prayer will bring kingdoms, thrones, and dominions down on their knees in awe of the great God. Prayer will destroy the works of darkness. Prayer is the key to a successful and victorious Christian life.

On the other hand, Prayerlessness Without Ceasing will cost you more than a few sleepless nights. This epidemic can cost you your ministry, your family, your children, your business, your job, and a lot more.

I plead with you today to begin a consistent and intense prayer life—for yourself, your family, your church, your city, your community, and your nation. I challenge you to pray for other nations throughout the world. Your prayer has much power. You can make a difference, and you can start right where you are. The following prayers will help you on your way.

This is a prayer for Ministers to pray for women as the spirit of God leads.

In the name of Jesus, I demand, command, and decree your release from every yoke, bondage, imprisonment, and every soul tie. I command you to be untied from that which has you bound through the witness of the blood of Christ. I declare that your soul is the Lord's. I command the chains around your hands, feet, and neck to be broken off you. I command walls of confinement to fall. I command you to leap over walls that have resisted you all these years. May you run through every troop and in the name of Jesus I confer upon you fresh oil, fresh power, supernatural power of deliverance, and of new beginnings.

I confer upon you that miracle of divine protection, deliverance, provision, and favor. I command a new stirring of God within your spirit man. I command you to rise up and take hold of God as never before. I reinstate your prayer life and spiritual sensitivity. Before Heaven and Earth, I declare that nothing will take your place.

Now lift your hands and pray this prayer with me.

Satan, take your hands off my life, my husband, my children, my home, my church, and my community. Take your hands off my inheritance, my finances, my health, my progress, my focus, and my prayer life. In Jesus' name, hands off! I will never be the same again. I will not be denied. I will see victory. I will see the salvation of my God in Jesus' mighty name.

"Classics by the Archbishop"
Purchase the whole book series today!

Divine Timing

The Price of Greatness

The Supernatural Power of a Praying Man

The Incredible Power of a Praying Woman

Praying Through the Promises of God

Destined to Make an Impact

Binding The Strong Man

Enforcing Prophetic Decrees

For more information on
Archbishop Nicholas Duncan-Williams
*and other powerful products,
please visit us online or contact
the office closest to you.*

AFRICA
www.actionchapel.net
Tel: + (233) 21.701.1851 (GHANA)

EUROPE
www.actionchapel.co.uk
Tel: + (44) 0208.952.0626 (UK)

NORTH AMERICA
www.prayersummitint.com
or call + (001) 202.587.2720. (USA)

Action Worship Center, Maryland
www.actionworshipcenter.net
+ (001) 301.498.7501

Action Chapel VA, Virginia
www.actionchapelva.org
+ (001) 703.224.8107

Lightning Source UK Ltd.
Milton Keynes UK
UKOW05f0605020717
304493UK00001B/6/P